Jairus

Copyright © 2001 Steve Applebee
All rights reserved.

ISBN 1-58898-555-5

Jairus

Steve Applebee

greatunpublished.com
Title No. 555
2001

Jairus

This book is dedicated to Natalie; my partner, my best friend, my inspiration, my passion, my wife.

Special thanks to my friends and teachers Dr. T.N. Redd and Dr. Frank McCoy.

CHAPTER ONE

In the early morning before dawn a light fog hung in the garden, like delicate damask draped between the ancient olive trees. Simon lay on top of a soft pile of leaves, his lamb's wool bedding thrown on top of the leaves and his blanket covering him, he was still more asleep than awake. He had a leather bag, that he carried his belongings in, under his head as a pillow and as he felt the softness of his pallet he thought of his wife. It had been too long since he had left home and, as he lay there in the coolness of the early light, his thoughts were of his family.

"You are going where? With whom, his wife had asked. "That's not even a little bit funny, Simon. A few days' fishing trip, well, that's our business, but this? Simon, you must be joking! You've been in the sun too long." That was her reply when he had told her of how Andrew had come to him that morning, more excited than he had ever seen him. Andrew had been in the highest of spirits, daily, since he had been following the Baptist. "We have found the Messiah!", Andrew came shouting, as he splashed through the shallow water out to Simon on his boat. For some time, Simon had been listening to Andrew's accounts of John's preaching and baptizing. He, himself, had even gone to hear and be baptized; and so Andrew's announcement did not come as a total surprise to him, for God had been speaking to his heart. However, Simon's declaration to his wife and family was a shock. Simon was a fisherman from Galilee, a businessman, and a good one, not a disciple of the Messiah. His wife was confused and afraid. What would become of their business? Of their security? Of their home? All these questions and doubts raced through her mind and out of her mouth as she realized Simon was serious. He was really going to leave everything and everyone to follow this Jesus. "What makes you think he is the Christ?" she had said, "We have been looking for Him for generations. What makes you so sure that He is the one, so sure that you would leave all?" Those were the thoughts that had been going through his mind all day as well. He really didn't have a black and white answer for his wife either, except that he felt compelled to go. He must go. This was not the man he had pictured as being the Messiah, but Andrew had spent the night with him and had heard what The Baptist said about Him: "Behold, the Lamb of God, which takes away the sins of the world", openly declaring that this man was the Son of God. Simon knew that he must follow him.

Tears streamed down Simon's wife's cheeks and she started to plead with him not to go, and then Jesus entered her home, and her heart. He took her face in his rough, but gentle carpenter's hands and brushed away the tears with his thumbs. Then, taking her hands in his, he looked into her soul, and said, "Fear not, daughter, for because of your husband's faith, all of your needs will be met far more than you could ever imagine." And she knew it would be so. "Now," said Jesus, "take me to your mother, I understand she needs some attention." The next morning they left Simon's home, and as they prepared to go, Simon's wife had given him the lamb's wool pallet that he now caressed as he lay beneath the shelter of the olive tree.

Praise God that their travels brought them back to his own doorstep relatively often, for he loved his wife and family dearly. That love gave him strength to continue, seeing them prosper in his absence. And he was not celibate like Jesus; he needed the companionship of his wife, as the temptations of a life in many cities and many temples were abundant. Her scent was on his pallet now, and it gave him comfort. From where Simon lay he could see Jesus' silhouette through the fog. This garden was their favorite place to camp before they entered this city. Now Jesus was kneeling next to a large rock, his arms outstretched toward heaven, the glow of the anointing of God shown round about him through the fog. It was Jesus' custom to rise before dawn to pray, and often he would ask Simon and the others to come and pray with him. But the days were long and hard and their bodies and minds weary, and they would not rise to be with him. Simon would watch him, though, as he wandered between waking and dreaming and would marvel at this man that he called "master".

"What do you see when you pray there, Master?" Simon asked him, once. "I see the events of the day unfold before me, as if I were remembering them from yesterday", Jesus replied. "I give praise, and honor, and thanksgiving as I seek the face of my Father; and I pray for you and your family, Simon."

So it was this morning, as Jesus rose from his place near the rock. Simon arose as well, and as Jesus approached, he felt deep satisfaction in their friendship. They embraced, and then went to awaken the others. Jesus turned in the now-clear garden morning, and pointed at the stone where he had been praying.

He said to Simon, "There you are my friend. Cephus! A stone; a rock among

men." Jesus had called him this since they first met. Simon still didn't understand what he meant by this, but he liked being called a "rock". He remembered Abraham being called a rock. Jesus smiled, laughing joyfully, as he knelt to wake John.

CHAPTER TWO

Jairus rose from where he had been kneeling on his prayer rug, most of the night. He looked out the window. The morning fog was just beginning to lift. In the distance, through the fog, he could see the dark walls of the city. The walls had always given him a sense of security. Within them, he knew that he was safe. Within them, he always knew where he was. In the darkness of the night past, he had risen once and looked out of this window and could not see the walls. Fear had briefly crept upon him, until a cloud passed from in front of the moon. Its light glistened off the stone of the wall, and peace returned to his mind. The fruit trees and shrubs of his garden were coming into focus, and he could see the shimmering drops of dew on their leaves. The moist grass was yet untrodden. Such a feeling of peace had not been upon his spirit since the morning that his daughter had been born, and he knew that all would be well. However, there was much to be done this day, and the Lord had given him clear instruction.

As Jairus looked out of the window into his garden, his thoughts returned to the night past. He had kissed his wife, and stroked her long, dark, hair; and had taken a moment, once again, to appreciate her beauty. The words of King Lemuel came to his mind nearly every time that he looked at her. Surely, this was a virtuous woman, and he was richly blessed. He then bent to stroke his daughter's brow, as her head lay in his wife's lap. Her forehead was cool. Her face ashen. Jairus prayed that he would once again see the soft peach glow of her cheeks, on top of her flawless olive skin. Emotion welled in his throat, and his eyes watered. He kissed his daughter on the forehead, touched his wife's shoulder, and hurriedly left the room. This was the worst that she had ever been, and fear had begun to come upon him. Jairus rushed down the hall and into his garden room, as if something were pursuing him. He flung himself desperately on his prayer rug, and this is where he had spent the night; rising only to lift his hands and heart in praise and thanksgiving to God. God had been faithful, as always, to speak to his soul. He had felt the Spirit of God near to him, and he knew that His kingdom: His love, His peace, His joy, His righteousness, was close at hand. His thoughts were than turned to Jesus.

Jesus had come to preach, teach, and heal in Jairus' temple. Well…it was God's temple…but he was ruler of this temple, and so he felt a sense of ownership, being its guardian. Like most people, Jairus was amazed at Jesus' doctrine and his authority. He truly admired this mighty man of God, even considering that he might be more than just a prophet. He had heard that the Baptist had called him the "Son of God". Could this be so? He had most often pictured the Messiah as Jeremiah had described him: a mighty warrior, coming to conquer Rome and set Israel up on high, not this shepherd of men. When Jesus spoke, however, the presence of the Lord was always evident.

Jairus' thoughts then returned to the last time that Jesus had preached in the temple. He told a story that Jairus had heard hundreds of times, and now that story seemed prophetic. Jairus had never considered the story quite the way that Jesus told it.

Jesus had told the story of the Shumanite woman. He read the account in the Scriptures, of how this well-to-do woman befriended the prophet Elisha, and gave him food and shelter whenever he was in her area. Elisha, in return for her continued kindness, prophesied that she would have a son, and she did. The boy grew, and one day, was with his father in the field. They were working with the reapers, when he injured his head. The father commanded that he be taken to his mother. He was carried to his mother, and he sat on her lap until noon, and then he died. The Shumanite woman laid the boy on the bed that the Prophet Elisha slept on when he was in their home, and then quickly went to find Elisha. As she approached, Elisha saw her coming in the distance. He sent his servant, Gehazi, out to meet her and ask: "Is it well with you? Is it well with your husband? Is it well with your child?"

That part of the story was the same for Jairus, but what Jesus said next in his lecture in the temple shed new light on the story. Jesus said, " Notice this woman's confession, and her reply to her husband, and to Elisha's questions brought by Gehazi. She said to her husband, "It shall be well." and to Gehazi, "It is well." She would not allow any negative confession to pass her lips. This woman showed her faith by what she spoke. She held at bay spiritual forces of death, speaking into existence spiritual forces of life. Her son's life was in her mouth. Did not Solomon say, "The power of death and life are in the tongue"?

The rest of the story was familiar to Jairus. Elisha went to the Shumanite woman's house, and raised the boy from the dead. It was this revelation that brought Jairus such peace, during his night of prayer in his garden room, and now he knew what he must do this morning.

CHAPTER THREE

Sarah hugged her pillow tightly. It was soft and warm, but she shivered. She was cold and alone. The room was dark, and she had no more oil for the lamp. No more oil. "That's all right", she thought, "The night is nearly past, and soon it will be light once more, and I will have another day." She caressed her pillow with her thin hand, and her long, raven-black hair almost cased the pillow. As she lay there in the darkness of her bedroom, her thoughts returned, once more, to her husband. How long had he been dead now? Her eyes closed but they darted from side to side, as she searched her mind for how long she had been without her man. The best that she could calculate was a little over twelve years. "My! How the time slips away", she thought, "What a man he was!" A smile crossed her lips, and tears welled up in her eyes. He was a short, burly man, with thick strong hands and powerful legs. He didn't have much hair, but he had the longest eyelashes of anyone she knew. His eyes were twinkly and soft...a light blue, like a spring sky. And oh! What a businessman he was too. He loved everyone, and everyone loved him, and everything that he had set his hand to had prospered. He had left her comfortable in her widowhood. She was left with a nice house, servants, and enough money to keep her comfortable for the rest of her life. That was unless something unforeseen should happen.

Sarah rose, wrapping her blanket tightly around her thin shoulders. "They were not always so thin," she thought. She made her way from the bedroom, through the darkness of the house. Even without the light, she knew the way, and there were not many things left to stumble over. There was a chair on the porch, and as she huddled under her blanket, she took her seat, drawing her knees up to her chest. This was one place where she still could find comfort, and her thoughts could come clearly. Her mind took her back to the time when it all had started. As she stared into the pre-dawn darkness, there were no morning shadows yet. A heavy fog was all that broke the blackness in front of her. Her thoughts drifted back in time, to just after the death of her beloved. She could see the events of that time, even now, despite what was before her eyes.

"Words. How powerful. How creative, or destructive. Blessings and cursings arise forth and issue from the lips, setting in motion things wonderful and things awful", she thought. She had almost passed the time of mourning, almost eased past the loneliness that she felt, and the missing of his voice and his steps in the house. Her friend had meant well, she thought; although looking back, she now questioned that belief. Oh, what her words had started. A simple comment, apparently uttered in passing, had planted a seed of fear in Sarah's heart. "I knew a woman once, who had lost her husband, although I don't recall how. Even though she was well off materially, the loneliness and pressures of being a widow became the death of her. I hope that this won't happen to you." In all of her time of mourning, Sarah had not taken time even to think of such things. Then, and still today, those words...simple, apparently innocent, echoed in her mind, locked in as if there were no escape. Then it had started, at first, just part of her normal cycle. But then worry and fear set in, and it became a flow of blood that no cure, no sacrifice, no money could stop. Now this morning, she had no more oil.

As she shivered, her mind came back to the present, and her eyes focused on the breaking of the first light. Fruit trees and shrubs in her yard became silhouettes, and the night fog began to lift, leaving behind heavy drops of dew on the grass. Almost as if it were audible, she heard a voice say, " Think on this." She was not startled by this voice, nor did she move to see where it had come from. Instead, she felt suddenly warm, as familiar objects in her yard began to take shape in the morning light. Peace and comfort were close at hand, and she could feel their nearness. "Think on what?" she questioned. "On what?" then she thought about Jesus, the prophet and teacher from Galilee. She had been to all of the priests and doctors, and had spent all that she had. Then she heard about the miracles of this man, Jesus. Some were even saying that he was the Messiah, the Son of God. So she had decided to take a chance, although it wasn't a chance which could cost her her life, because he was preaching in the desert, and not in the temple. She would go see this Jesus. Still, she would be ridiculed if she were seen. She had covered her face and stayed back and away from any face that seemed familiar. Even as far away as she was she could hear this mighty man of God, as he preached as if to her ears alone.

"Blessed are the poor in spirit", he had begun, "For theirs is the kingdom of heaven. Blessed are they that mourn, for they shall be comforted." That was her! She was blessed! Oh, what sweet words those were. She then heard him say, "Ask, and it shall be given unto you. Seek, and you shall find. Knock and it shall be opened unto you. For everyone that asks, receives, and he that seeks, finds. And to him that knocks, it shall be opened".

"Oh, God", she prayed, "I'm asking! Seeking! Knocking! Please open the door, and heal me!" She thought that she felt at that moment, her flow of blood stop. She thought that she had received her healing, and for the first time in twelve years, praise came from her lips and heart. She had rushed back home, to show herself to the priest. However, instead of rejoicing with her, he scoffed at Jesus and his teachings. He rebuked her for going forth in the day, among others. Could he be right? Her fear crept back in. Shortly thereafter, her flow started again.

That was months ago, but yesterday, she had heard that Jesus was coming to her city. He would be there today, going to the temple to teach, preach, and heal, as was his custom. If she were caught in public, she could be stoned, but this was her last chance. She would be dead soon anyway. If she could only touch the hem of his garment, she would be healed. As the sun began to peek over the horizon, and the night' darkness began to fade, Sarah cast off her blanket and hurried inside to get ready to go to the city. "There will be a big crowd there, and I must get there early". "Thank you, God for your favor and mercy", she prayed, "I'm going to see your Son!" It was going to be a glorious day, and she set her face toward the city gates.

CHAPTER FOUR

Peter listened to Jesus, speaking to the disciples this morning, preparing them for the day ahead. He was always so encouraging...so uplifting, and there was always a smile on his face, and a twinkle in his eyes. Except, that is, when he spoke with the Pharisees. Peter thought of the months past, and the work that had been started. He had heard Jesus say that there was still much to do. It seemed as though Jesus slept less and less these days, as his ministry, and the people, required more and more of him. Yet, when Peter asked Jesus about this, he told him, "Peter, we shall run, and not grow weary. We shall walk and shall not faint, for the Lord will go before us, and His joy shall be our strength." Jesus kept his thoughts, his actions, his words and his prayers in the right now. His vision was always before him. He was the most focused person that Peter had ever met.

Peter thought back to the first time that Jesus had spoken about His purpose. Jesus had come to Nazareth, where he had been brought up. As was his custom, he went into the synagogue on the Sabbath and stood up to read. There was delivered to him the book of the prophet Isaiah. When he had opened the book, he found the place where it was written, " The Spirit of the Lord is upon me, because he has anointed me to preach the gospel to the poor; He has sent me to heal the broken hearted, to preach deliverance to the captives, and recovering of sight to the blind, to set at liberty them that are bruised. To preach the acceptable year of the Lord." Then he closed the book, and he gave it again to the minister, and he sat down.

Peter had heard that the men of the synagogue had gotten so mad at Jesus, after his reading, and what he had spoken to them concerning the condition of their hearts, that they tried to throw him off a cliff. He had just walked through the midst of them, however, and went his way. Peter thought of how Jesus was anointed by God, with the Holy Ghost, and with power. How he went about doing good, and healing all that were oppressed by the devil, for God was with him. Peter was a witness to all this that he did. That thought brought goose bumps to his arms, and tears to his eyes. He knew how blessed he was to call this man, this Son of God, "friend". He would recall this thought later, but this morning he had more immediate things to occupy his mind.

He and Jesus, and the rest of the disciples, had camped in this olive grove the night before. It was good shelter, secluded enough, and yet not far from the water. They had crossed over the lake in the fog, and the townspeople had not yet noticed that they were there. So as the morning sun began the new day, they had been able to sleep undisturbed. They had even had a good breakfast before word began to spread that Jesus was near. Even though there were plenty of first rate accommodations for them in the city, Jesus loved sleeping among the olive trees best. This suited Peter. The crowds had grown so large, and so demanding of Jesus and his time. These days it seemed that Peter spent much of his time, just keeping Jesus from being mobbed. At least, he felt that he was good at that. And so, this morning, as they began to prepare for the day ahead, they held hands and joined their spirits as Jesus prayed for them and those that they would minister to this day. When their prayer was finished, their hearts pounded like the drums of Rome. Their hands and feet were full of energy, and their souls were full of rejoicing. Jesus led them, as he strode towards the city. His long bronze legs were strong and muscular, his shoulders were broad, and his eyes were alive with love. He began to sing a song of David, singing, " Oh Lord, our Lord, how excellent is your name in all the earth! Who has set your glory above the heavens..." Peter had to run to catch him.

CHAPTER FIVE

Jairus waited and watched from the temple steps for his servant to signal him that Jesus was approaching. His palms were moist in anticipation, and his large nostrils flared to bring in oxygen enough to supply his anxious heart. His arms were crossed above his surprisingly lean belly. Even though he was only forty, many of his peers in the religious community who were close to his age had waists of prosperity. Despite his position and power, Jairus worked diligently not to be a hypocrite, to speak well of and do good to all who were in his charge, and to please God. His dark eyes fixed on the city gate, which he could see well from the temple steps where he stood. His servant's signal came, as the streets of the city began to come alive with the sounds of morning. The crowds began to make their ways to their early destinations. Jairus took the temple steps two at a time, as he strode, unimpeded, toward the city gates. Gone were the thoughts that he could lose his position for this action that he was taking and gone were the worries of what others might think. He focused on his daughter, on his wife, on his words, and on Jesus. He would not be denied. All was well.

CHAPTER SIX

When Sarah arrived at the city gate, Jesus had just entered. The crowd was already so large that she saw no way to get to Jesus. At first, panic had gripped her mind, and then her heart sank as she saw her life being carried away by the throng. But hope returned as the crowd stopped and parted...as though a wedge had been driven into it from the front, straight toward Jesus. The disciples fought to make a way through the crowd so that Jesus could get to his destination, the temple. Sometimes, it seemed as though the crowd would suffocate them. Sarah climbed up on a nearby wagon to get a better view, and to see why the crowd had stopped and parted.

To her astonishment, she saw Jairus, ruler of the synagogue, striding toward the healer. Jairus' servants pushed the crowd away from the front, and the disciples kept them away from the sides. She thought, "This is how it must have looked when Moses parted the Red Sea." Then the people gasped, almost as if they were one person. Jairus had thrown himself as Jesus' feet! Sarah knew that this would be her last and only chance. Quickly, she climbed down from the wagon. She was still quite agile, despite her infirmity.

Asking to get through the crowd, or even pushing seemed to do her no good. The people seemed compressed... like a wall. Determination rose up within her. All the years of frustration and isolation burst forth from her. She would not be denied this time. Sarah dropped to her knees, and began to crawl toward Jesus. She picked her way diligently, between the sea of ankles and sandy feet.

Moments seemed like hours, as she got kicked and stepped upon. Finally, she could see Jesus, and he had not yet moved.

Jairus had walked confidently toward Jesus, and the crowd, recognizing their ruler, had given way. None of them had expected what they saw next. Jairus threw himself prostrate at Jesus' feet, in total submission of authority. After their initial gasp, the crowd fell hushed and silent, as they waited to see what would happen next. That is, all except one.

Sarah knew that this was her only chance. She must reach Jesus now, or all would be lost. Gone were the thoughts of fear, gone was the worry about tomorrow. Right now was all that she had. Her dress was ripped at the knees, from crawling across the stony ground. The palms of her hands bled, and her knuckles were already swollen and red from being stepped upon. She noticed none of this though. With dust in her eyes and mouth, she focused in desperation on the hem of Jesus' garment. She moved with surprising speed as the crowd, for an instant seemed to part for her, to get to the one who could save her life.

Jesus bent and touched Jairus on his shoulder, and gently helped him to his feet. Jesus knew this man well, and he liked him. This man was one of the few men in the religious community who Jesus felt was truly seeking the Father. Jairus was doing the works that showed that he was both humble of heart, and upright of character. Jesus knew what Jairus was risking by throwing himself at his feet this morning, and he appreciated his faith. He seldom saw it in a man of Jairus' position. The cares of this world and the deceitfulness of abundance often choked the word of God from their hearts, and their works became unfruitful. Had he not just spoken of that very subject to the multitudes and to his disciples?

Jairus stood upright now, but he still had to lift his eyes to look Jesus in the eyes. But lift his eyes he did, and as he did, in his mind the crowd seemed to melt away. The peace that passes any understanding rose up within Jairus and as Jesus held him close with a hand on each shoulder. Jairus spoke what was in his heart. "Master", he said, "my little daughter lies at the point of death; please, I pray you, come and lay your hands on her, that she may be healed; and she shall live." Seconds seemed to pass by as if they were minutes for Jairus just then. No one spoke, no one moved, it seemed as if no one even drew breath. All seemed as if it were in slow motion, until Jesus said, "Come". He pulled Jairus close to him, and they turned to go to Jairus' house. Time felt as though it had broken free with the word "come", and everything returned to its normal fast pace. It staggered Jairus a little, and had Jesus not held him by the shoulder, he may have fallen back into the crowd. The crowd quickly closed in around the two men and neither Jesus' disciples nor Jairus' servants could hold them back. There was a surge of movement... a pulse...and engulfing wave of people that threatened to suffocate those caught in its wake.

Sarah had seen her chance. As Jesus and Jairus turned to go, and the crowd moved with them. Sarah used their forward momentum to push her, and she lunged toward her goal. With a desperate plunge, her thin hand caught the contact point of her faith, the hem of his garment. Jesus felt a tug on the hem of his garment. This could have been the crowd just stepping on it, but Jesus felt more than just a tug on his robe, he felt someone's faith. He felt that faith, a very real force, pull the anointed healing power out through him.

CHAPTER SEVEN

Jairus' wife sat nearly motionless, lovingly stroking her daughter's hair. How much like her own it was, long and dark as ebony. Her mind drifted back to the birth of her sweet little one. My! What a wonderful time that was. What joy and celebration they all had. How grown she seemed now, lying here, with her head in her mother's lap, and the length of her body stretching toward the end of the bed. She was becoming a woman. It seemed like just yesterday that she was still bathing her and watching her take her first steps. Her little hands and feet were so cute! Now they were almost as big as hers. "Please God, let my baby live!", she pleaded. She knew that Jairus had gone to get Jesus, and she also knew that she must hold fast to one thought, "All is well".

Her attention was pulled away from the cold pallor of her daughter's face by a soft knock on the bedroom door. Her maidservant stepped into he room, and bowed slightly. "Mistress", the servant girl asked, " Is there anything that I can bring you?" "No thank you", she replied absently, "All is well". The servant girl stepped nearer, and looked closely at the lovely young maid, lying motionless on her mother's lap, colorless and cold.

Puddles of tears welled up in the eyes of the servant girl. This child was her friend, and now she was...she didn't want to even think about it. Her eyes met the eyes of the girl's mother, searching for reassurance, comfort, strength. Jairus' wife's eyes met the young girl's panicked eyes with a fixed and focused intensity. "Send word to Jairus to hurry! Now!" she said forcefully.

The servant girl hesitated briefly to gaze a moment more at the seemingly lifeless girl on the bed before her. She spun quickly out of the bedroom, moving toward the kitchen, deep in thought. She knew that there she would find the manservant, who was in charge of carrying messages for the household. She stepped into the kitchen, struggling to contain her emotions, and found him, finishing his breakfast. When she gave him the message, he asked, " Is she much worse?". She could contain herself no longer, and burst into sobbing. "Is she dead?, he asked. She only repeated the message, and said again, "Tell Jairus to hurry!" The maidservant did not know this member of the household well, he had only been with them a short time. He had come to her master from the Temple, where he had worked for one of the Pharisees. It was imperative that all messages the he carried be relayed exactly as they were given, and so his was an extremely important and delicate job. His memory must be sharp and his character true. In the short time that she had known him, he seemed reliable enough, but she was not yet settled about his loyalty to her master.

"She's dead isn't she?" he queried again. "I knew that Jairus was wasting his time going to see that Jesus this morning. His time would have been better spent preparing for her funeral!" The maidservant, at this statement, regained her composure and repeated her mistress's words, "All is well". "I'll go get Jairus", he said, snatching another warm piece of bread from the cook's tray. "Tell him to hurry. That's all", she said sternly.

This messenger had his own idea, though. He had worked in the Temple for many years before he had recently come to work for Jairus. His former master had not always spoken highly of this ruler of the Temple...he wanted his job. This Pharisee believed that Jairus was not using the power of his position appropriately. Jairus was too sympathetic, too forgiving...not legalistic enough. He was too generous with his praise and his purse...especially since Jesus had been teaching, preaching, and healing in the Temple and all over Galilee. In this man's opinion, if Jairus did not better conceal his admiration and respect for Jesus, he would lose all control. The loyalty of this servant still lay with his previous employer, and he had been carefully watching Jairus, and faithfully reporting all that had been transpiring in his household, and in his dealings in the community.

"This is a perfect opportunity", he thought, "The girl is dead, and Jairus has risked everything by going to Jesus. Now my former master will be ruler of the temple, and I will be exalted." He finished his bread, and as he passed through the courtyard, he began to tell some of the other servants about the girl's death, and they began to wail and mourn. Many of the servants of Jairus' household had been with them since before the girl's birth, and they all loved her dearly. On the way to the city gates, the messenger stopped by the temple to tell his former master of the situation. "I will send the musicians to the house", the Pharisee said, with a slight smile turning up one corner of his mouth. He raised an eyebrow and told the servant to go tell Jairus.

CHAPTER EIGHT

Sarah could feel her issue of blood stop immediately, as she touched the hem of Jesus' garment; just as it had that day when she had heard him speak in the country. Jesus stopped suddenly, as he felt Sarah's faith pull her healing from his anointing. The crowd pressed even more tightly around him and Jairus. It was all that the disciples could do to keep them from being crushed. Sarah got to her feet quickly, successfully melting into the crowd, unnoticed. Jesus looked around, searching the eyes of the people near him-not in anger, but in love; not in rebuke, but in surprise that someone's faith had touched him so strongly. Jesus said, "who touched me?" Everyone who was near denied it. Peter and the others who were with him said, "Master, this multitude throngs you and presses you, and almost suffocates you; and you say 'who touched me?.

Jairus stood patiently next to Jesus, saying nothing, but watching intently. Jesus said, "Somebody touched me: for I perceived power going out from me." He looked around again, into the windows of the souls surrounding him to see who had done this thing. Then his eyes met Sarah's. He could see the anointing still strong upon her. It was so strong and fresh that he could smell it.

Sarah knew that she could not hide; and strangely, she really didn't want to. She came trembling toward Jesus, as the crowd eased its press, and parted for her to make her way toward him. She fell down before him and wept at his feet. His strong and gentle hand first touched her head, and then her thin shoulder, which shook with her weeping. He reached for her arm and helped her to her feet. Jesus looked softly at her, and smiled.

With no hesitation, and no trembling in her voice she said, "Master, I came here today because I have had an issue of blood for twelve years. No doctor could cure me; in fact I've gotten worse, and no priest could heal me. I have spent all of my money, and now there is no more oil . I said to myself, that if I could but touch the hem of your garment, I would be healed. And so it was. Praise God! I'm healed!". Jesus drew her close and hugged her. When she looked into his eyes, she could see them dance and sparkle. He said to her, "Daughter, be of good cheer; your faith has made you whole. Go in peace." He kissed her forehead, and turned her in the opposite direction that he and Jairus were going. Releasing her, he turned to Jairus and smiled, patted him on the back, and they turned to go.

Sarah's feet barely seemed to touch the ground, as she made her way through the crowd that was once again in motion with Jesus. As she reached the back of the crowd, she noticed that it had stopped again already, but there were too many people in her way for her to see or hear the reason why they had stopped. Now that she had cleared the throng, and taken a moment to pause, she rejoiced. She jumped into the air and spun around. For the first time in twelve years, she was well and happy! Tears of joy welled up in her eyes, and she smiled nearly from ear to ear. As she paused, she took a moment to examine herself. The scratches and cuts that were on her hands, knees, feet, and face were also gone, and there was no pain anywhere in her body. Her eyes were as clear as they had been when she was a child. She was overwhelmed with gratitude. Not only had Jesus not had her stoned (which was his right and authority, because she was in a public place with her affliction) but he had made her completely whole. He had not only healed her issue of blood, but had restored every fiber of her depleted and tired body. By calling her "daughter", Jesus restored her into the community again. She was dazed with delight!

As she turned to go, she was surprised to see that some of the other women broke from the crowd, and turned to go with her.

Noticing the puzzled look on her face, one of the women spoke before Sarah even had a chance to. "We heard you say that you had spent all of your money, and that there was even no more oil. We have come to help."

Even as Jesus was finishing speaking with Sarah, the messenger from Jairus' house came hurriedly up to them. Pushing and shoving his way through the crowd, he stopped directly in front of Jesus and Jairus. The forward momentum broken, the crowd began to press in once more, and the disciples had to use all of their strength and experience to keep the mass of people from crushing in upon them. The servant, relishing this moment, had a veiled expression of mockery on his face. He looked first to Jesus, and then to Jairus, and said, " Your daughter is dead. Do not trouble the teacher any further." This was not news to Jairus, considering his daughter's condition when he had last seen her and the time that had passed since his early morning departure. Without his speaking with his mouth, Jairus' expression spoke volumes. He looked first at the servant with anger, for sowing seeds of doubt. His heart and his look then turned to pity, as he realized that this man was merely without any faith. Jesus turned to Jairus, and said, "Do not be afraid; only believe, and she will be made well."

"Come", he said to Jairus, and stepping around the stunned and silent servant, they moved once more to Jairus' house. Jairus thought, "All is well." As they passed by the temple on the way to Jairus' house, Jesus stopped and asked the crowd not to follow them any farther. He permitted only Peter, James, and John to come along.

CHAPTER NINE

After the five men passed the temple, and the throng stayed behind, Jairus relaxed a little. There were a few moments of quiet now, before they reached his house. He noticed that the sun was now well up, and that the sky was a crisp blue. The clouds, like sheep, were moving lazily as the breeze that touched his face. It was a large day. His feet knew the way to his house from where they were, even if it had been pitch dark. His mind then, free to wander, took a short journey down another road. They were not far from his house. Jairus and Jesus walked side by side, with Peter, James, and John a few paces not far behind. Jairus stayed close to Jesus, so close that several times their shoulders touched. Their strides were long. Their pace urgent, but not alarmed.

Jairus thought, "Who is this man that I walk beside? Who is he really? Is he the son of God? Is he really the Messiah?" He thought about the stories that he had heard, stories of the miracles of his birth and youth. He remembered the slaughters of Herod, nearly thirty years before. Jairus had been just a lad then, just coming into manhood. He had heard of how Jesus taught in the temple at Jerusalem, at the age of twelve. He knew how most of the Pharisees felt about Jesus, and how Jesus had always rebuked them for their hypocrisy. Jairus had even heard Jesus preach in the temple that he was ruler of. "Surely", he thought, "this man is the son of God." "But he is so different from what we had all expected. If someone had asked me to list the characteristics of the Messiah before I met Jesus,

I doubt that they would have matched him." The next question that popped into his mind was, "But what do the scriptures say about the Messiah?" As he began to search the scriptures in his mind, his memory did not take him to a specific passage, but he remembered hearing once from one of his teachers, that all scripture pointed toward the Messiah.

Just as his mind began to focus on a particular scripture, he was reawakened to the present situation by the sound of loud music coming from his house. Someone had summoned the professional mourners, and they were already there, playing the flute and wailing for the dead. "Professional mourners", he thought, "I never realized how morbid they were until this moment." Now they made him want to rend his garments and to tear at his hair. Peace was restored to him quietly, by a gentle pat , and a strong hand on his back. Jairus remained silent. His face was set; his mind focused. "All is well", he thought.

There was a considerable tumult in front of his house. Peter thought, " If someone didn't know the circumstances, but saw this crowd, they would know that something very tragic had happened in the life of someone very important." Jesse's pace picked up, as he neared the outer courtyard. There were people outside, as well as inside, the house. Jairus stayed by Jesus' shoulder.

The mourners outside saw Jairus coming, and they turned to greet and comfort him. Jesus strode through their midst. Jairus was at his side, not looking or responding to their wailing, except to say, "Make room". In just a few strides, they were at the entrance to the house. Peter, James, and John were close behind. It was like the priests crossing over the Jordan River.

Before the crowd had a chance to collect their thoughts, Jesus stopped in the doorway and asked, "Why make this commotion and weep? The child is not dead, but sleeping." For an instant, everyone was in shocked silence. They all looked at Jesus in astonishment, and then they looked at each other, and the silence broke. "How do you know", said one, "you just got here." Someone else said, "We know that word was sent to Jairus, did it not arrive?" As a chorus, the crowd then began to ridicule and mock Jesus.

"Out!, said Jesus, and with a quick glance toward Peter, he stepped inside. Peter quickly set about getting them to leave, even as far as the outer courtyard. Peter liked this type of work and he was good at it. John quickly and efficiently found the mother and the room where the child was lying. Jairus stepped securely to his wife and embraced her, holding her tightly as he felt her sob. He held her in silence for a long moment as Peter, James, and John cleared the house. Jesus waited, a faint smile was on his lips and fire in his eyes.

Jairus loosed his embrace, stepped back and took his wife by the shoulders to look in her eyes. Tear trails decorated her cheeks. She was pale and in her eyes there was concern. But she was a warrior and this was her child. She believed in her husband and she knew that he believed in Jesus. Straightening herself, she wiped the tears from her cheeks and looked first at Jairus, and then at Jesus. "All is well" she said as she turned her gaze once more upon her daughter. It was a look that only one that had given birth could give, full of tenacious love, compassion, and a total unwillingness to compromise to death. John saw this look and thought that it was interestingly like many he had seen on the face of Jesus.

Jesus smiled broadly and enveloped her in a big carpenter's hug. A peace like she had never known caressed her mind and relaxed her body. Color came back to her cheeks. She recognized the feelings she was having. She hadn't felt like this since the day her daughter was born. Jesus looked deeply into her eyes; he was still smiling and his eyes danced with light. They looked at where her daughter lay pale and still. The six of them entered the room like an invading army. The windows had been closed and the room was dimly lit by candles. John quickly opened every window and light flooded in filling the room. Jesus stepped away from the others and stood beside the motionless child. He gazed softly at her for a moment. She was beautiful, much like her mother. He could see the strength of youth and character in her form. Love and compassion poured forth from his entire being like rivers of living water. Then he took the child by the hand and said to her, "Little girl , I say to you, arise". Jairus didn't know if it was from the light outside or if it came from Jesus, but it was so bright in the room that he could barely see what happened next.

The sweet, gentle breeze that had blown across his cheeks earlier swept through the room. His daughter's gown rustled with the breeze and immediately she arose and walked. She smiled at Jesus as he held her hand and looked into her eyes. Then his glance went to Jairus and her mother. The girl turned her eyes to follow his gaze and her smile grew as she saw her parents. Her mother saw the beautiful rose of her daughter's cheeks and the life in her eyes. Jairus had to steady her for a moment because she was almost overcome with joy. Then, like a flash, she rushed to her daughter and hugged her as she had never hugged her before. Jairus stepped to his wife and daughter and embraced them both. Jesus said to John "Get her something good to eat." John and James both left the room to find the kitchen and retrieve the cook. Jesus stepped aside with Jairus and his wife for a moment. "You must tell no one what happened here this morning", he said. "Now, let's all go and have something good to eat."

The news of the miracle had already begun to spread, as fast, it seemed, as the cool breeze that had blushed their cheeks earlier. Jesus would have much to do the rest of the day. He got a brief respite before he left Jairus' house. He readied himself for the glorious task of undoing many of the works of the enemy, and magnifying his Father. Jairus asked Jesus, "How do you do it? How do you continually pour so much of yourself into the people?" Jesus smiled broadly, his eyes alive. He squared his shoulders and lifted his chin. He spread his long, tanned, muscular arms full span and said, "They that wait upon the Lord shall renew their strength; they shall mount up with wings as eagles; they shall run, and not be weary; and they shall walk, and not faint. The Lord goes before me and His joy is my strength." He wrapped one arm around Jairus' shoulder and gave him a short hug. Then, he began to laugh, joyously, heartily. His laughter was contagious and shortly everyone was laughing so much that their jaws ached and their breathing seemed to come in gulps.

Jesus instructed Jairus to stay with his family as he prepared to leave the house. Before he left, however, Jairus asked Jesus to return for the evening meal. Jesus agreed and Jairus watched him as he turned and left until he was no longer in sight. Jairus was struck by the strength of his stride, the bounce in his step, and the authority of the anointing that carried Jesus. He knew that goodness and mercy followed this man all the days of his life and all that he set his hand to prospered. Then, he raised his eyes and his voice to heaven and glorified God and thanked Him for Jesus' presence in his life.

CHAPTER TEN

When Jesus returned to Jairus' house he was not surprised to find his two good friends Joseph of Aramathea and Nicodemus there. For some time, they had been traveling with Jesus, going into whatever city or part of the countryside Jesus visited. Jesus considered Joseph a disciple. He and Nicodemus were known at the gates of every city in Galilee. Jesus loved them both, and was pleased to see them here. John had come with Jesus and when he saw these two men of the Sanhedren he knew that this would be a special evening. John felt a ripened expectancy hanging in the air, like grapes hanging from a vine, as they entered the house. "This is going to be good" he thought to himself, and a smile graced his lips.

As they entered the house Jairus stopped near the doorway. There was a basin of water there, a cloth, and a vial of oil. He knelt and washed Jesus' and John's feet and dried them and then arose and anointed their heads with the oil. Jesus knew that Jairus had the heart of David, a heart after God's own heart. They all embraced and Jesus and John followed them to the room in which they were to sup. It was a comfortable room; rich tapestries, made by Jairus' wife, hung on the walls, and rugs from Persia covered the stone floor. Large pillows lay behind low tables. Here they could relax, sit or recline, and fellowship shoulder to shoulder, and eye to eye. John thought, "This beats fish on a fire pit any day! Although that's not bad, this is better by far." He settled on a pillow near the corner where he could watch and listen. He knew there were men of wisdom and experience in this room and he wanted to see and hear it all.

They ate fruit and nuts and drank red wine. They talked of their experiences and of people they knew. They ate bread sopped in venison stew and they laughed at stories that Jesus told. They relaxed and enjoyed each other's company as men. Jairus recounted the day's events, and then, as it seems to happen at times like these, there was a lull in the conversation. It was not an uncomfortable silence. On the contrary, they all gazed contentedly at the tapestries and smiled peacefully in their comfort. John lifted his eyes, from where he had been looking at nothing in particular, and looked at Jesus. He sensed the evening was going to change direction. His feelings were not disappointed.

Jesus leaned close to Nicodemus, put his hand on Nicodemus' forearm and smiled slightly, looking at him softly in the eyes, and asked, "Who do people say that I am"? Nicodemus thought for a moment, his mind traveling back over the past months since he had first met Jesus one night in the garden, near his home. He thought of the places he had been since then. He had followed Jesus into cities and the country, talking to people that Jesus ministered to, taught and preached to. People of both high station and those who were outcasts. "Truly," Nicodemus thought, "all the books in the world could not hold in their pages all that he had seen Jesus do and say". "Most", he said in response to Jesus' question, looking into Jesus' eyes and seeing there a peace that passed all understanding, "I think you are a great prophet and healer, like Elijah or Elisha".

Jesus leaned yet a little closer to Nicodemus and said "Who do you say that I am"? Every eye in the room fixed on Nicodemus and all their hearts pounded strongly in their chests. What a question! Had they not all, at one time, asked themselves this question? But they had not ever confronted the question fully personally. Now they faced the question from Jesus himself. Jairus felt goose bumps run up his spine and down his arms. The hairs on his arms stood erect, and the back of his neck tingled. It seemed to him that he could feel every hair on his head. His head felt light, almost as if he had had too much wine, but his senses were all on alert.

Tears of joy rose in his eyes. Had he not just asked himself this question earlier this day? He watched intently, as Nicodemus briefly lowered his eyes in thought, and he leaned forward on his elbows to hear Nicodemus' reply. The air was thick with anticipation. Nicodemus looked back into Jesus' eyes. He grabbed both of his hands in his own, and said, " By all that I know, all that I have seen, all that I have heard, and by all that I have read in the scriptures; you are the Messiah."

"He said it!, Jairus thought, and almost leapt to his feet. "He said it! A man of wisdom, and knowledge, and learning." Glory to God! Someone other than himself felt that way! Jairus was so happy that he felt that his spirit might leave his body. Joseph was feeling likewise. He leaned forward on the table in front of him, grasping its edges and trembling with excitement. Nicodemus squeezed Jesus' hands, and sat back on his pillows. He was almost stunned at what he had heard himself say; but very much at peace with it. He knew that he had prophesied.

Jesus smiled, and turning to Joseph of Aramathea, his disciple he said, "Who do you say that I am?" Joseph pounded the table in front of him, with his open hand, leapt to his feet as if he were a young man, and rushed to Jesus, pulling him to his feet. He embraced Jesus. Then loosing his embrace, and flushed with emotion, with tears of joy on his face and excitement in his voice he said, "You are the Christ. The anointed one. You are the Son of God." Joseph raised his arms, jumped up and down, and spun around rejoicing. He embraced Jesus again, and then flung himself on his pillows, with the exhaustion that follows intense excitement. He was nearly unconscious with happiness.

Finally, Jesus turned to Jairus, who had also risen to his feet. Jairus had heard the testimony of his two friends. He felt in his heart exactly as they did, and he was eager to reply. Jesus looked into Jairus' eyes and Jairus felt the presence of God, stronger than he had ever felt it before. Jesus waited for an instant. Time seemed suspended. Once again a silence filled the room, and all eyes fixed on the two men of God, facing each other. Jairus had the words on his tongue that echoed those of Nicodemus and Joseph, but they did not exit his lips. His mouth opened, then it closed. His eyes dropped from Jesus', and they darted from side to side along the floor as if following the progress of a rabbit. He felt all of the blood rush from his face. He paled and trembled, and a look of horror replaced the look of exultation that had just been on his face. His eyes met Jesus', and tears of sorrow streamed from his eyes, leaving their traces on his cheeks. Jairus felt like his mouth had filled with sand, and he wanted to retch.

Jesus held his eyes with his, and they filled with compassion. He grasped his friend's shoulders with his strong carpenter's hands, and smiled easily at Jairus. " Tell them what you know", Jesus said softly. Nicodemus looked at Joseph, and Joseph at Nicodemus. They both looked at Jesus, and at Jairus, and then back at each other. The anointing that had been present only seconds ago, but which seemed like hours ago now, was replaced with momentary confusion. John sat silently in the corner and watched and listened. Once again their eyes returned to Jesus and Jairus. Jesus grasped Jairus' other shoulder and Jairus felt like a priest entering the holy of holies. "You must speak what you know" Jesus said again to Jairus, "All is well."

Jairus felt moisture return to his mouth and throat and the blood return to his face. In the instant that Jesus had looked at him, before he could speak the words of praise that were in his heart, he had remembered the scripture that had briefly come into his mind earlier in the day. They had been interrupted by their approach to his house and by the noise of the mourners but now they came to him as clearly as if the book were open in front of him. Jairus did not want to speak them but Jesus compelled him to. "What does the prophet Isaiah have to say about the Messiah, Jairus?" Jesus asked. Jairus realized that Jesus knew what had shaken him so. Realizing that Jesus knew, however, did not make speaking the words any easier.

Jesus raised an eyebrow and withdrew his hands from Jairus' shoulders, and said, "Speak, Jairus". And so Jairus spoke. "Who has believed our report? and to whom is the arm of the Lord revealed? For he shall grow up before him as a tender plant, and as a root out of the dry ground: he has no form nor comeliness: and when we shall see him, there is no beauty that we should desire him. He is despised and rejected of men: a man of sorrows, and acquainted with grief: and we hid as it were our faces from him: he was despised, and we esteemed him not. Surely he hath borne our griefs and carried away our sorrows: yet we did esteem him stricken, smitten of God, and afflicted. But he was wounded for our transgressions, he was bruised for our iniquities: the chastisement of our peace was upon him; and with his stripes we are healed. All we like sheep have gone astray; we have turned everyone to his own way; and the Lord has laid on him the iniquity of us all. He was oppressed, and he was afflicted, yet he opened not his mouth: he is brought as a lamb to the slaughter, and as a sheep before her sheerer is dumb, so he opened not his mouth. He was taken from prison and from judgment: and who shall declare his generation? for he was cut off out of the land of the living: for the transgression of my people was he stricken. And he made his grave with the wicked, and with the rich in his death; because he had done no violence, neither was any deceit in his mouth. Yet it pleased the Lord, to bruise him; he has put him to grief: when you shall make his soul an offering for sin. He shall see his seed, he shall prolong his days, and the pleasure of the Lord shall prosper in his hand. He shall see of the travail of his soul, and shall be satisfied: by his knowledge shall my righteous servant justify many; for he shall bear their iniquities. Therefore will I divide him a portion with the great, and he shall divide the spoil with the strong; because he has poured out his soul unto death: and he was numbered with the transgressors; and he bare the sin of many, and made intercession for the transgressors."

Jairus staggered backward a couple of paces. He slapped both hands over his mouth as if he were trying to keep any more words from coming out of it. He not only knew what he had just heard himself say, he understood the implications of this scripture. He was very confused. Floods of thoughts washed across his mind and they seemed to be coming in such torrents that he couldn't make sense of them. Tears returned to spill out of his eyes and his nose started to run. Only one thought, one word, was Jairus able to get an anchor on. He steadied himself on a nearby table and with trembling lips asked Jesus —

"Why?"

Joseph had listened intently to the scripture that Jairus had quoted. He too was well familiar with it, but until this very moment, he had not related the words of Isaiah to this man, Jesus. Even though he had been with Jesus for some time, and many of the things that he said seemed strange, this revelation was by far the most shocking. Joseph backed into a corner, horrified, weak-kneed and trembling. He remembered a report he had heard about what Caiaphas, the high priest, had said. Caiaphas said, "You know nothing at all, nor do you consider that it is expedient for us that one man should die for the people, and not that the whole nation should perish." Now this he did not say on his own authority; but being high priest that year he prophesied that Jesus would die for the nation, and not for that nation only, but also that he would gather together in one the children of God who were scattered abroad.

Nicodemus slumped back onto the cushion he had risen from and stroked his beard introspectively. A light of revelation shone in his eyes. Jesus once again moved close to Jairus, wrapping an arm around his shoulder as if he were tucking him under a wing. He looked over his other shoulder at Nicodemus, and knowing his thoughts, saying, "Tell us why Nicodemus." Nicodemus smiled. Something had troubled Nicodemus since the night he had first met Jesus. It was something Jesus had said and Nicodemus had followed him from that time until now hoping to find the answer. Now he had it! He remembered that encounter like it had just happened. He had come to Jesus at night, in secret, because Jesus was very unpopular with his Pharisee brethren and he did not want to be seen with him. Nicodemus had heard Jesus preach and teach and had seen him heal and he knew that he was a man of God. A simple yet profound question was on his mind, and he came to Jesus in respectful submission, hoping to find an answer. "What must I do to enter the kingdom of heaven?" was the question that was in his heart and on his mind.

He had not even spoken the words yet but Jesus knew that this was the reason Nicodemus had come to him. Jesus felt that Nicodemus was one of the few of his order who was truly seeking God and His truths. What he said next Nicodemus had meditated on everyday since then, and he knew the words by heart. Jesus had said to him "Most assuredly, I say to you, unless one is born again, he cannot see the kingdom of God." Nicodemus said to him, "How can a man be born when he is old? Can he enter a second time into his mother's womb and be born?" Jesus answered, "Most assuredly, I say to you, unless one is born of water and the Spirit, he cannot enter the kingdom of God. That which is born of the flesh is flesh, and that which is born of the Spirit is spirit. Do not marvel that I said to you, ' You must be born again.' The wind blows where it wishes, and you hear the sound of it, but cannot tell where it comes from and where it goes. So is everyone who is born of the Spirit."

Nicodemus answered Jesus and said , "How can these things be?" Jesus answered and said to him, "Are you the teacher of Israel, and do not know these things? Most assuredly, I say to you, We speak what We know and testify what We have seen, and you do not receive Our witness. If I have told you earthly things and you do not believe, how will you believe if I tell you heavenly things? No one has ascended to heaven but He who came down from heaven, that is, the Son of Man who is in heaven. And Moses lifted up the serpent in the wilderness, even so the Son of Man be lifted up, that whoever believes in Him should not perish but have everlasting life. For God did not send His Son into the world to condemn the world, but that the world through Him might be saved. He who believes in Him is not condemned; but he who does not believe is condemned already, because he has not believed in the name of the only begotten Son of God. And this is the condemnation, that the light has come into the world, and men loved darkness rather than light, because their deeds were evil. For everyone practicing evil hates the light and does not come to the light, lest his deeds should be exposed. But he who does the truth comes to the light, that his deeds may be clearly seen, that they have been done in God."

Nicodemus repeated this conversation now for all to hear. Jairus listened quite like Nicodemus had when Jesus said these words to him. He thought about these words, his eyes lowered, once again chasing the thoughts that seemed to be trying to escape. He thought of the words of Isaiah, that he had just spoken. He tried to piece them together, as obviously, Nicodemus had. Jairus hadn't had the time to meditate on these words as much as Nicodemus had though, and he couldn't seem to make the connections. It was just too much, too fast. He said to Nicodemus, "Please, explain these things to me." Joseph had worked his way to a cushion to listen. John took mental notes. He knew that he was witnessing events like none other in the history of man. His young mind was like a blank tablet for these events to be written upon.

Nicodemus began, " Let's begin with what we know. First, man must believe that God is, and that He is a rewarder of those who diligently seek Him. Next, man has to believe that God created him in His image and gave him dominion over the earth. Finally then, man must believe that the first man, Adam, abdicated the authority that God had given him to Satan, through lack of faith and disobedience. It was a princeship gained through treachery and deceit yet never-the-less obtained. Hence, the breaking of the covenant between God and man. We have been spiritually dead ever since, in that, we have been born from the seed of Adam. Abraham regained and restored the covenant through faith. The animal sacrifices performed from that time until now, were only temporary coverings for our sins. God, I believe, wants to allow for the remission of our sins completely, once and forever. To do this, a man must be offered up, and not just any man, but a sinless man. Only a man born of incorruptible seed, not born of man, but supernaturally conceived by God's Holy Spirit could accomplish a sinless life. I believe that Jesus is this man. I believe that he will be lifted up as Moses' serpent, and I believe that He will die a death that will cover all men's sins, if they will believe that He died for them. I believe that He will be raised from the dead, and that He will live again. Just recently, I heard Jesus say to the Pharisees, 'Destroy this temple, and in three days I will raise it up.' To believe that Jesus will die for our sins and is the Son of God will restore our rightstanding with God; not because of what we can or cannot do, but because of what He has done for us. We will be 'born again' of the Spirit. Even as He will be the first born, a new creation, so will we be like Him. We will live forever, and see and enter the kingdom of God. Hallelujah! Thank-you Jesus!"

Jesus returned his eyes to Jairus and said, "Who do you say that I am Jairus?" Jairus was sobbing now, fully realizing the impact of what he had just heard. He pulled himself up, squared his shoulders, wiped his nose and eyes, and looked deeply into the eyes of the man who he knew was the Messiah, the Son of God. His voice still shook some, more perhaps from excitement now rather than from sorrow. He said "I believe Jesus, that you are the Lamb of God." Jesus pulled Jairus close and hugged him tightly, then he pulled back slightly and kissed him on both cheeks, smiling broadly, his eyes dancing.

"Is there anything we can do?" came a voice from a nearby corner. Joseph asked again "What can we do Lord?" Jesus still smiled; it was a smile that awakened dreams in men's hearts, a smile that would light the world. "There will come a time Joseph, when I will ask something of you. I will ask something of you and those here tonight and I will ask something of all men who choose to believe on me. But now is not the time for those things to be spoken of. Now is the time to sit together once more. It is the time for us to fellowship, to eat and drink, and to sing. Tomorrow will come, and bring with it its troubles. But fear not, for I have overcome the world. Now, let's rejoice, sing psalms and worship the Lord."

As they sat once more Jesus began to sing, "Blessed is the man who walks not in the counsel of the ungodly, nor stands in the paths of sinners, nor sits in the seat of the scornful: But his delight is in the law of the Lord, and in His law he meditates day and night. He shall be like a tree planted by the rivers of water, that brings forth its fruit in its season, whose leaf also shall not wither; and whatever he does shall prosper."

THE END

ABOUT THE AUTHOR

born-1956 in Hastings,Ne1956-1968 lived in Hastings,Ne1968-1970 lived in Rabun County,Ga1970-1974 lived in Clay Center,Ne1975 lived in Fountain Inn,S.C. and graduated from Hillcrest H.S.1975-1979 attended The Citadel in Charleston,S.C.graduated from The Citadel in 1979 with a B.A. in Englishmarried Natalie Lima in 1984twin girls born in 19851984-present work for UPS1987-present live in Summerville,S.C.

ABOUT GREATUNPUBLISHED.COM

greatunpublished.com is a website that exists to serve writers and readers, and remove some of the commercial barriers between them. When you purchase a greatunpublished.com title, whether you receive it in electronic form or in a paperback volume or as a signed copy of the author's manuscript, you can be assured that the author is receiving a majority of the post-production revenue. Writers who join greatunpublished.com support the site and its marketing efforts with a per-title fee, and a portion of the site's share of profits are channeled into literacy programs.

So by purchasing this title from greatunpublished.com, you are helping to revolutionize the publishing industry for the benefit of writers and readers.
And for this we thank you.

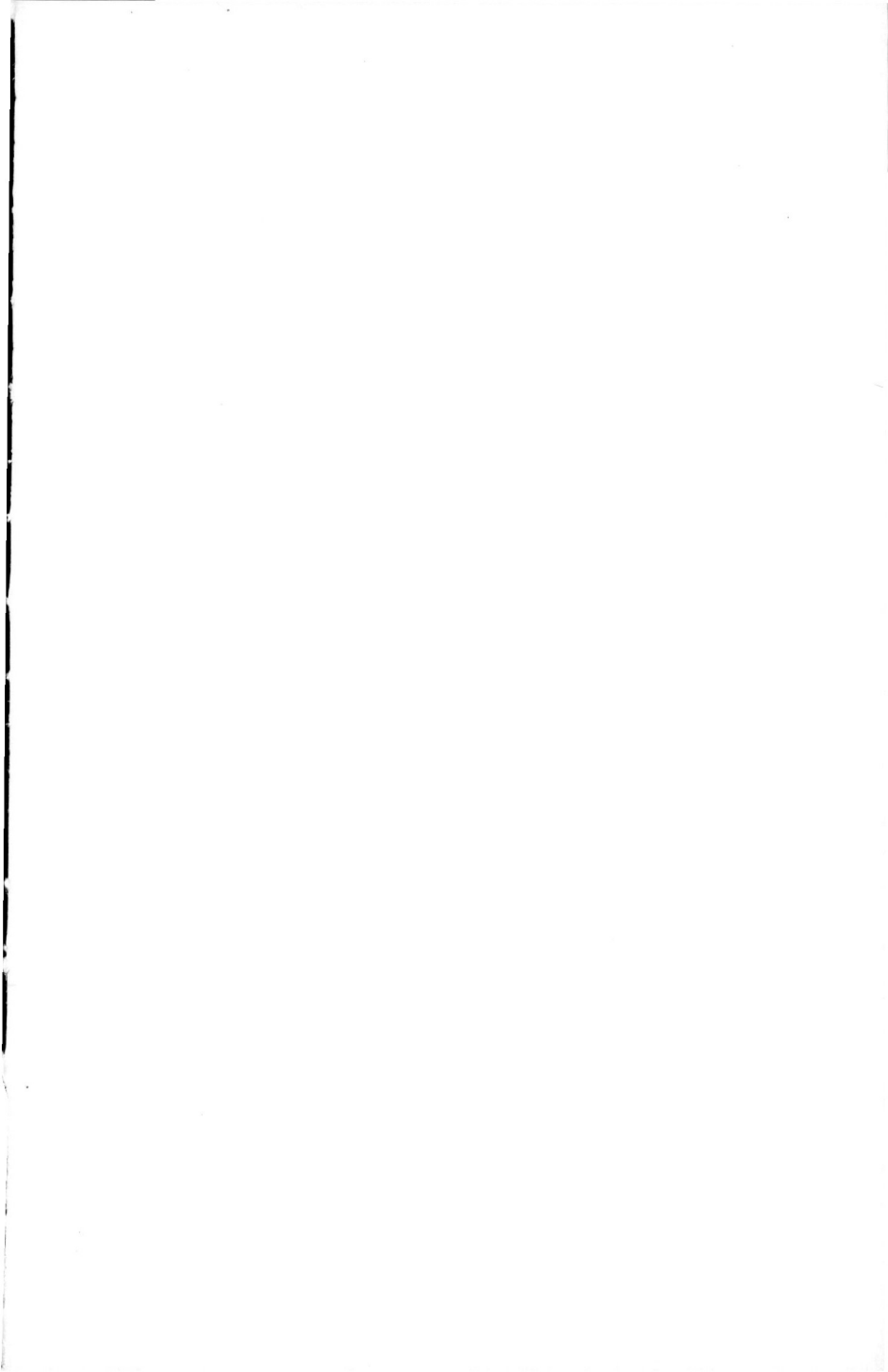

Made in the USA
Columbia, SC
28 April 2023